KEVIN VON ERICH:

The Legend of Texas

Wrestling

Shirley S. Kelley

DISCLAIMER

The following book is for informational purposes only. The information presented is without contract or any type of guarantee assurance. While every caution has been taken to provide accurate and current information, it is solely the reader's responsibility to check all information contained in this article before relying upon it.

Neither the author nor publisher can be held accountable for any errors or omissions. Under no circumstances will any legal responsibility or blame be held against the author or publisher for any reparation, damages, or monetary loss due to the information presented, either directly or indirectly.

Trademarks and pictures are used without permission. Use of the trademark is not authorized by, associated with, or sponsored by the trademark owners. All trademarks and pictures used within this book are used with no intent to infringe on the trademark owners and only used for clarifying purposes.

This book is not sponsored by or affiliated with KEVIN VON ERICH, it is just his detailed biography from a very reliable close source, or anyone involved with him.

TABLE OF CONTENTS

INTRODUCTION

The sweat and thunder of the wrestling ring produced a mythology deep in the heart of Texas, where the sun scorches the plains and the stars shine brightly at night. Here, in the land of dreamers and oilmen, cowboys and cattle, the Von Erich family name became a byword for wrestling royalty. One individual stood out among the sons of this legendary dynasty, not because of his extraordinary athletic ability or his golden hair that glistened like the sun over the Lone Star State, but rather because of his unwavering spirit in the face of unfathomable sorrow. This is the story of Kevin Von Erich, the warrior who performed acrobatics and remained grounded in his native red earth while reaching the pinnacles of wrestling fame.

The narrative of Von Erich's ascent and subsequent grief is woven into the very fabric of Texas wrestling. It is a story that enters fans' hearts and minds all across the globe in addition to the squared circle. In addition to the burden of expectation, Kevin, the third child of wrestling pioneer and patriarch Fritz Von Erich, also bore the history of a family that had come to embody the sport in the South.

This book will take us on a tour through the sacred halls of wrestling history, following Kevin Von Erich's career from the beginning, when he was still learning the ropes from his father and competing against his siblings, to the breathtaking pinnacles of his time spent as a lone wrestler. From his daring dropkicks to his mastery of the Iron Claw—a technique that became a Von Erich trademark that was both feared and admired in equal measure—we will revisit the thrilling moments that catapulted him into the public eye.

But in order to comprehend Kevin, one also has to comprehend the shadows cast by the Von Erich moniker. The personal setbacks that would have crushed a weaker man, but which Kevin bravely endured to motivate everyone around him. His tale is not just one of physical prowess but also of an unwavering determination that lifted him out of the pit and enabled him to battle on—not only for himself but also for his family's history.

This is not only a book about wrestling. This tale revolves on a family, love, and an unbreakable spirit. It is a tribute to the everlasting spirit of Texas wrestling and the fans who supported the Von Erichs through good times and bad. You will experience the intensity of the limelight, the thunderous applause of the masses, and the unwavering bond of blood and sweat that typifies Kevin Von Erich's life as you flip these pages.

Get ready to face a legend, experience the force of history in your hands, and learn about the life of a man who rose to prominence as a hero and a representation of the resilience of the human spirit. This is the story of Denton County native Kevin Von Erich, the barefoot youngster who rose to become the undisputed champion of the Texas wrestling industry.

CHAPTER 1: EARLY LIFE AND BACKGROUND

Kevin Von Erich, a former professional wrestler and part of the renowned Von Erich wrestling family, was born Kevin Ross Adkisson on May 15, 1957. Though his father, Jack Adkisson, better known as Fritz Von Erich, was a professional wrestler and promoter in Denton, Texas, he was born in Belleville, Illinois.

Of his six brothers, Kevin was the second oldest; all of them would go on to become professional wrestlers. Kerry, Mike, Chris, and eventually Ross, his younger brothers, all pursued their father's career as professional wrestlers, as did their elder brother David.

Kevin and his siblings were big fans and participants in professional wrestling when they were little. Frequently, they would accompany their father to wrestling matches and assist with ring setup. Kevin and his brothers also received training at their father's wrestling academy, where they were taught the fundamentals of the art.

Kevin had different interests at first, despite his family's wrestling participation. He was a gifted athlete who participated in basketball and football in high school. He was a guitarist in a band and had a strong love for music.

Nevertheless, Kevin ultimately made the decision to follow in his father and elder brother's footsteps and seek a career in wrestling. When he made his professional wrestling debut in 1976, he was only 19 years old, and he immediately won over the fans.

Both triumph and tragedy characterized Kevin's wrestling career. His high-flying, acrobatic approach earned him several titles. But he also had many injuries, such as an ACL tear and a fractured neck.

Kevin lost his three brothers, David, Mike, and Chris, tragically, at a young age from a variety of circumstances, including drug overdose and suicide. Due to consequences from a motorbike accident, Kerry also passed away at an early age.

Notwithstanding these unfortunate events, the Von Erich wrestling family continues to rank among the most well-known and significant in professional wrestling history. Due to their contributions to the sport of wrestling, Kevin and his surviving brother, Ross, have left a lasting legacy in the business.

Growing Up in a Wrestling Family

The most recognized aspect of Kevin Von Erich's career is his time spent competing in World Class Championship Wrestling (WCCW), where he was a successful member of the Von Erich family. Kevin's upbringing was profoundly impacted by being from a wrestling family; it shaped his career and fostered deep relationships and sibling rivalry among the brothers.

Kevin Von Erich was the second oldest of the five Von Erich brothers; Kerry, Mike, and Chris came after David.

Their father was the renowned professional wrestler and promoter Jack Adkisson, also known as Fritz Von Erich. Fritz started WCCW, which in the 1980s rose to prominence as one of the biggest wrestling companies in the US.

Kevin and his brothers were introduced to the professional wrestling industry at an early age due to their family's involvement in the sport. They saw their father's commitment to the sport, which inevitably shaped their own goals. Growing up, the boys saw their father compete in the ring, absorbing all of the industry's nuances and developing a profound passion for the sport of wrestling.

With the help of their father, the Von Erich brothers trained and improved their wrestling abilities as they got older. Fritz thought his boys had what it took to continue his legacy and saw promise in them. Kevin and his brothers began participating in regional competitions, where they progressively acquired expertise and notoriety.

Any family may sometimes have conflicts between siblings, but in the Von Erich home, the rivalry reached new heights. The brothers were vying not only for the admiration and approval of their father but also for the attention and devotion of the supporters. Due to the distinctive styles and personalities of each brother, there were often fierce rivalry between them both inside and outside the ring.

Among the Von Erich brothers, the rivalry between Kevin and his younger brother David was the most prominent. David gained popularity fast and was regarded as the most gifted and endearing of the brothers. David and Kevin were competitive as a result, with Kevin seeking to outdo his brother and establish his own reputation.

The Von Erich brothers had a close relationship in spite of their rivalry. As members of a wrestling family, they were aware of the difficulties and sacrifices involved. Through wounds, misfortunes, and internal turmoil, they

14

provided mutual support. In addition to being teammates, the brothers were also closest friends and confidants.

The Von Erich family has gone through a lot of losses and difficulties. Acute enteritis claimed David Von Erich's life in 1984, leaving his family devastated. Kevin and his brothers experienced a profound loss that strengthened their bond. They came to understand the value of cherishing their relationship and standing by one other at the most trying moments.

Following the death of his brother David, Kevin Von Erich's career as a wrestler went on. He was a huge success in the wrestling world, taking home several titles and earning a lot of respect. But Kevin's emotional and mental health suffered as a result of the traumas and losses. In order to devote more time to his family and personal life, he ultimately made the decision to leave professional wrestling.

Being one of the most recognizable people in professional wrestling history, Kevin Von Erich's legacy continues to this day. The continuing spirit of the Von Erich name and the strength of family are shown by his narrative of growing up in a wrestling family, facing sibling rivalry, and creating unbreakable relationships with his siblings.

CHAPTER 2: TRAINING AND WRESTLING DEBUT

As a member of the illustrious Von Erich wrestling family, Kevin Von Erich, a former professional wrestler, rose to stardom. The well-known wrestler and promoter Fritz Von Erich is his father, and he is the brother of other wrestlers David, Kerry, Mike, and Chris Von Erich. Fritz Von Erich, Kevin's father, had a significant impact on both his training and wrestling debut. Fritz Von Erich was instrumental in molding Kevin's career.

Under the careful supervision of his father Fritz, Kevin Von Erich started his training at an early age. Kevin was exposed to the ins and outs of the wrestling industry at a young age since he grew up in a home where wrestling was prevalent. As a well-respected wrestler, Fritz shared his knowledge and experience with his son, making sure he got the finest instruction possible.

Kevin trained hard physically to build his strength, agility, and endurance under Fritz's direction. Kevin was instilled with the ideals required to thrive in the wrestling profession by Fritz, who stressed the significance of discipline and hard work. Weightlifting, aerobic workouts, and wrestling drills were all part of Kevin's training program. He was also taught the psychological side of wrestling by Fritz, who emphasized the value of audience interaction and narrative.

Fritz Von Erich exposed Kevin to a variety of wrestling styles and tactics, which was an important part of his wrestling education in addition to his physical preparation. Because of Fritz's extensive network of contacts in the wrestling business, Kevin was able to study under some of the top wrestlers of his day. Kevin would often get to spar with more seasoned wrestlers, which gave him priceless in-ring experience and improved his technique.

On August 17, 1976, at the age of 19, Kevin Von Erich made his debut in professional wrestling. In front of an enthusiastic audience anxious to see the Von Erich family's next generation in action, he made his professional wrestling debut in Dallas, Texas. Both spectators and other wrestlers praised Kevin for his first bout, which displayed his natural agility and technical skill.

Kevin Von Erich's wrestling style was greatly impacted by his father Fritz during his career. Fritz had a reputation for taking a tough, no-nonsense approach to wrestling, and Kevin followed suit. His distinctive and captivating in-ring image was created by combining technical wrestling with daring techniques. Kevin's fights were known for their high-risk maneuvers and vicious brawls, which captivated crowds and cemented his place as a fan favorite.

Fritz Von Erich's impact went beyond wrestling technique and conditioning. As a promoter, Fritz was instrumental in starting World Class Championship

Wrestling (WCCW), a Dallas, Texas-based company. During the 1980s, one of the most prosperous wrestling companies in the US was WCCW, which Fritz led to great success. As the faces of WCCW, Kevin and his brothers drew sizable crowds and captivated spectators with their in-ring antics.

Outside of the wrestling arena, Fritz had a significant impact on Kevin Von Erich's career. He ingrained in Kevin a strong sense of duty, honesty, and dedication to his family. Kevin persevered and kept up his wrestling career in spite of the untimely deaths of his brothers David, Kerry, and Mike. By doing so, he upheld the Von Erich name and his family's heritage.

Father Fritz Von Erich had a big effect on Kevin Von Erich's training and professional wrestling debut. Fritz's advice, knowledge, and contacts in the wrestling world were invaluable in helping to mold Kevin's career. Under Fritz's guidance, Kevin blossomed into a gifted and esteemed wrestler, renowned for his distinct approach and fascinating exhibitions. Fritz Von Erich had an impact on Kevin that went beyond wrestling because he taught him the principles that are essential for success in both the ring and outside of it.

Training with World Class Championship Wrestling

Early in the 1980s, Kevin Von Erich, a professional wrestler, received training from World Class Championship Wrestling (WCCW). Of the Von Erich brothers, a wrestling family well-known for their accomplishments in the sport, he was the second oldest.

Under the direction of his father, Fritz Von Erich, Kevin started his training with WCCW in 1980. Fritz, a former professional wrestler, started the WCCW in 1966. He was well-known for his severe training regimens and didn't think any less of his own kid.

Kevin was committed to succeeding despite his demanding and taxing training. He practiced his skills and picked up new ones in the ring for hours on end. He also focused on improving his physical fitness by jogging and lifting weights to increase his stamina and strength.

After competing in his first WCCW contests in 1981, Kevin gained recognition in the wrestling community very rapidly. He was renowned for his graceful movements and his capacity to engage the audience. In the ring, he was an expert technician as well, easily pulling off difficult moves.

Kevin's 1982 victory over the NWA American Heavyweight Championship was one of his early victories. In a fierce battle that demonstrated his abilities and tenacity, he prevailed against Gino Hernandez. Kevin's rise to prominence in the wrestling industry was solidified with this triumph.

Following that, Kevin had several more lucrative fights with WCCW, one of which being a legendary rivalry with Ric Flair in 1984. In addition, he joined forces with his brothers Kerry and David to create the renowned Von Erichs tag team.

Kevin's wrestling career was not without its difficulties, even with his successes. He was forced to miss time from the ring due to many injuries, including a fractured ankle and a torn bicep. Along with these personal difficulties, he battled despair and drug addiction.

Kevin maintained his popularity in the wrestling community in spite of these difficulties. In 1995, he announced his retirement from professional wrestling, although he kept appearing at conventions and matches. In order to assist others, he also turned into an advocate for mental health awareness, sharing his personal experiences with addiction and sadness.

Though hard and demanding, Kevin Von Erich's training with WCCW equipped him for a successful career in wrestling. His early achievements, such as winning the NWA American Heavyweight Championship, solidified his position as a rising talent in the professional wrestling industry. Kevin overcame numerous obstacles to maintain his status as a revered figure in the wrestling industry and to this day, his advocacy work inspires others.

CHAPTER 3: THE RISE OF THE VON ERICHS

In the 1970s and 1980s, a renowned family of professional wrestlers came to prominence: the Von Erichs. Kevin, David, Kerry, and Mike were the four brothers who made up the family and all of them were very successful professional wrestlers. The Von Erichs were renowned for their physical prowess, charm, and capacity to enthrall crowds with their daring stunts and fierce rivalries.

The Von Erich family's ascent started in the 1960s when their father, Fritz Von Erich, started competing in Texas wrestling. As a prosperous wrestler and promoter in the state, Fritz cultivated a devoted fan base. Though he had six boys, only Kevin, David, Kerry, and Mike pursued professional wrestling careers.

In the realm of wrestling, the Von Erich brothers gained notoriety quite fast. They were renowned for their attractiveness, athleticism, and fan-friendly demeanor. Intense rivalries with other wrestlers, especially the Fabulous Freebirds, a trio of wrestlers from Texas, were another aspect of their reputation.

Throughout the 1970s and 1980s, the Von Erichs' popularity increased. In Texas, they quickly gained widespread recognition and became household names. Among the many titles and honors they garnered were the Texas Heavyweight Championship and the NWA World Tag Team Championship.

But catastrophe did not accompany the Von Erichs' victory. David Von Erich passed away from acute enteritis, a rare intestinal illness, in 1984 when he was only 25 years old. Kerry Von Erich had a similarly terrible end when he overdosed on drugs in 1993 and lost his foot in a motorbike accident.

The Von Erichs' legacy endures in spite of these catastrophes. They are among the all-time great wrestling families, and their influence on the sport endures to this day. The Von Erichs' success may be attributed to their skill, diligence, and love for what they do. In the realm of wrestling, they will always be regarded as legends.

Individual Feuds and Tag Team Success

Pro wrestler Kevin Von Erich is a renowned figure who had great success in tag matches as well as solo feuds. He is considered by many to be among the most well-liked and well-known professional wrestlers in Texas history. He and his family, who went by the moniker "the Von Erichs," rose to prominence in the sport.

When Kevin Von Erich and his brother David Von Erich forged a strong alliance in the early 1980s, their popularity as a tag team took off. The team, dubbed the

"Texas Broncos," emerged as the NWA American Tag Team Champions on many occasions and gained rapid notoriety in the organization. Fans flocked to their battles because of their high-flying, hard-hitting style and indisputable synergy in the ring, which made them favorites.

Kevin was grieved and the wrestling community was shocked by the tragic death of David Von Erich in 1984. Kevin kept up his impressive tag team performance in spite of this devastating loss, joining forces with his two brothers, Kerry and Mike, to carry on the Von Erich heritage. After winning several titles and enthralling crowds with their exciting battles, the Von Erichs came to be seen as the epitome of tag team perfection.

The Fabulous Freebirds, a competing group fronted by Michael "P.S." Hayes and Terry "Bam Bam" Gordy, were the subject of one of Kevin's most notorious feuds throughout his career. Fans from all around Texas and beyond were enthralled with the Von Erichs and Freebirds' fierce rivalry. Their conflicts included pride, honor, and the heritage of their families in addition to titles. When Kevin beat Hayes to win the NWA World Heavyweight Championship at the legendary "Parade of Champions" event in 1984, the rivalry reached its zenith and sent the fans into a frenzy.

Kevin was the most well-liked person in Texas. The Texans looked up to the Von Erichs as heroes, not simply as wrestlers. Their relationship with the fans extended beyond the squared circle because they embodied the spirit and ideals of the Lone Star State. Fans packed the stadium to see their beloved heroes compete during the Von Erichs' historic battles in the Dallas Sportatorium, setting attendance records.

The untimely death of many Von Erich brothers, including David, Kerry, and Mike, served to reinforce the legendary reputation of the family and the strong emotional connection between the Von Erichs and their followers. Kevin persevered in wrestling and inspiring others with his unyielding attitude, despite the heartache and personal challenges. He remained a symbol of tenacity and persistence.

Wrestling history, especially in Texas, would not be the same without Kevin Von Erich's successful tag team career and his solo feuds. He had a lasting impression on the business with his alliances with his brothers and his conflicts with competing groups like the Fabulous Freebirds. The success of the Von Erichs in Texas was a result of their extraordinary skill, magnetic personality, and close bond with their fans. Fans everywhere will always remember and respect Kevin's legacy as a wrestling star and his contributions to the sport.

CHAPTER 4: TRAGEDY STRIKES

Six brothers, all of whom wrestled professionally, made up the Von Erich family, a well-known wrestling dynasty in the 1980s. But tragedy befell the family when Mike, Kerry, and David, the three brothers, all passed away at an early age.

The first to go away was David Von Erich, who died in 1984 at the age of 25. He was on the edge of becoming a big star in the business and was regarded as the family's most gifted wrestler. While on tour with All Japan Pro Wrestling, David was discovered dead in his hotel room in Japan. Though a drug overdose was suspected to be the cause of death, the official cause of death was stated as acute enteritis. The family and the wrestling community as a whole suffered a terrible loss with David's passing.

The next to pass away was 23-year-old Mike Von Erich in 1987. His own wrestling career had been cut short by a shoulder injury, and he had battled addiction and melancholy since the death of his brother David. After taking an excessive amount of the pharmaceutical sedative Placidyl, Mike was discovered dead at his parents' Texas house. They declared his death to be a suicide.

The last of the brothers to pass away, at the age of 33, was Kerry Von Erich in 1993. In addition, he had battled addiction and suffered a foot loss in a 1986 motorbike accident. In 1990, Kerry emerged victorious from the World Wrestling Federation Intercontinental Championship, having persevered in wrestling despite his disability. But his private life was in disarray, and in 1992 he was arrested for drug possession. With a gunshot wound to his chest, Kerry was discovered dead at his father's Texas house. He was also declared to have committed suicide.

The wrestling world lost a family that had provided so much thrills and entertainment when David, Mike, and Kerry Von Erich passed very tragically. The family lost three cherished sons and brothers due to tragic circumstances surrounding their deaths, and they were left to mourn. The fans' recollections of the Von Erichs endure, as does the sport and entertainment business's sustained appeal in professional wrestling.

Coping with Loss and Continuing the Legacy

Over his life, Kevin Von Erich has experienced a fair amount of loss. Kevin had to deal with a great deal of sadness and figure out how to carry on the Von Erich family heritage after the untimely loss of his siblings and personal hardships. His wrestling career has greatly benefited from this experience, which has made him the strong, resilient person he is today.

With Kevin and his brothers Kerry, David, Mike, and Chris all becoming well-known in the professional wrestling industry, the Von Erich family was a wrestling dynasty. They were adored by the crowd and regarded as some of the most gifted and exciting wrestlers of their day. But the family was beset by catastrophe time and time again, and Kevin was left to deal with unfathomable grief.

The first setback occurred in 1984 when Kevin's brother David tragically departed away. As a rising star in the wrestling business, David's passing shocked everyone in the business. The death of his younger brother upset Kevin, and he found it difficult to accept that he would never see him again. Kevin had to find the will to go on without his brother at his side, which had a significant effect on his wrestling career.

When Kevin's brother Mike committed himself in 1987, tragedy hit once again. For Kevin and the Von Erich family, this tragedy was just one more tragic setback. During this period, Kevin went through unimaginable sadness and anguish, which negatively impacted his mental and emotional health. Kevin wrestled on, a way to respect his brothers' legacy and provide an outlet for his grief in spite of his deep sadness.

The most devastating loss Kevin experienced was the suicide death of his brother Kerry in 1993. Kevin was devastated by Kerry's passing since he was his lone surviving sibling. The loss was almost too much to take, and Kevin began to doubt both his own mission and the Von Erich family's history. He made the deliberate choice to continue the family's wrestling heritage, nevertheless, and refused to allow his sadness to overcome him.

Although dealing with such a significant loss is never simple, Kevin Von Erich has shown to be very strong and resilient throughout his ordeal. By using his suffering as motivation, he has made sure that his family's reputation endures in the professional wrestling community. Kevin has inspired a lot of people by demonstrating that it is possible to find the will to go on even in the face of unfathomable sorrow.

The defeats Kevin has suffered have had a significant influence on his wrestling career. He was forced to face his own mortality and consider the meaning of his work by the sorrow and suffering he went through. Kevin, however, embraced his wrestling career as a means of honoring his brothers and perpetuating their memories rather than giving up.

Kevin developed a more passionate and fierce wrestling technique in the ring. In an effort to respect the memory of his brothers who lost their lives, he put his all into every match. He was a fan favorite because of his tenacity and perseverance, and he gained recognition for his daring maneuvers and unwavering mindset.

Kevin has advocated for mental health and the value of getting treatment outside of the ring by using his platform. He has been transparent about his own grieving process and has urged people to ask for help when they do. Because of his openness and willingness to share his experience, Kevin has been an inspiration to many, demonstrating that even in the most difficult circumstances, it is possible to find purpose and strength.

Throughout his life, Kevin Von Erich has experienced great loss, yet he has overcome these setbacks with remarkable fortitude and fortitude. Despite how much his brothers' deaths have affected his wrestling career, he has channeled his sorrow into carrying on their legacy. Kevin's story demonstrates the strength of tenacity and the capacity to find meaning despite unfathomable loss.

CHAPTER 5: CHAMPIONSHIP REIGNS AND FEUDS

Kevin was a successful solo combatant and tag team wrestler with his brothers, belonging to the illustrious Von Erich wrestling family. His many title victories and captivating feuds during his career cemented his place as one of the most adored and esteemed wrestlers of his age.

Early in the 1980s, Kevin Von Erich won the NWA American Heavyweight Championship many times, ushering in his tenure as the champion. Kevin's triumphs demonstrated his amazing in-ring talents and agility, making this renowned championship one of the most sought for in the WCCW. His stints as the American Heavyweight Champion were characterized by fierce bouts with some of the best opponents in the league, such as "Iceman" King Parsons, "Gentleman" Chris Adams, and "Gorgeous" Jimmy Garvin.

Kevin Von Erich was a successful singles combatant, but he also made a lot of progress as a tag team wrestler. Together with his brothers, Mike, Kerry, and David, he formed The Von Erichs, a formidable combination in the tag team scene. The group demonstrated their remarkable chemistry and cooperation by winning the NWA American Tag Team Championship many times. They played some of the most memorable games in WCCW history, including ones against iconic teams like The Fabulous Freebirds and The Dynamic Duo (Adams and Gino Hernandez).

The battle between Kevin Von Erich and the Freebirds, which drew large crowds and shaped Texas wrestling culture, was one of his most memorable feuds. After the Freebirds assaulted the Von Erichs in 1982, there was a series of violent and very emotional bouts that resulted in the extreme hostility between the two groups. The conflict culminated in 1984's famed "Parade of Champions" event, when Kevin and Terry Gordy engaged in a historic match for the NWA World Heavyweight Championship. The encounter is still remembered as one of the most memorable in WCCW history, despite Kevin's failure to win the world championship.

Kevin Von Erich's singles accomplishments went beyond winning championships. He consistently competed for the NWA World Heavyweight Championship and often faced off against ex-champions Harley Race and Ric Flair in exciting matches. His battles against these elite wrestlers cemented his status as a major event class wrestler, even if he never won the world championship.

Sadly, personal traumas, such as the sudden deaths of his brothers David, Mike, and Kerry, tainted Kevin Von Erich's career. Kevin was so affected by these defeats that he decided to end his career as a professional wrestler in 1995. It is impossible to exaggerate his influence on the sector or his role in WCCW's accomplishments, nevertheless.

The title victories and feuds that Kevin Von Erich had were evidence of his extraordinary skill and commitment to the professional wrestling industry. His accomplishments in both solo competition and with The Von Erichs demonstrated his adaptability and capacity to succeed in a variety of settings. Kevin has had personal traumas, but his reputation as one of the best wrestlers of all time endures, and his influence on the wrestling industry will always be felt.

Memorable Rivalries with Wrestling Legends

Over the course of his remarkable career, Kevin Von Erich engaged in a number of notable feuds with legendary wrestlers. Kevin was a part of a wrestling dynasty that had a lasting impression on the business as a member of the renowned Von Erich family. Kevin's rivalries were a major factor in molding his career, and the Von Erichs have had a huge influence on professional wrestling.

The legendary "Nature Boy" Ric Flair and Kevin Von Erich had one of their most memorable rivalry. Their dispute demonstrated their amazing in-ring skills and captured the attention of viewers in the 1980s. Flair, who was renowned for his flashy appearance and technical skill, struggled against Kevin's natural strength and agility. Both guys pushed each other to the maximum throughout their hard-hitting, heated battles. Their rivalry for the NWA World Heavyweight Championship turned into a classic match, and their connection was evident.

Kevin will always cherish his feud with the illustrious "Rowdy" Roddy Piper. In contrast to Kevin's more restrained manner, Piper's boisterous personality and unconventional style were well-known. In addition to being physical, Piper would often use psychological tactics to obtain the upper hand in their conflicts. One of the bloodiest matches in wrestling history, the dog collar fight that capped off their animosity is still remembered.

A legendary rivalry existed between Dusty Rhodes, the "American Dream," and Kevin Von Erich. A charming and well-liked character, Rhodes provided the ideal counterpoint to Kevin's portrayal of the all-American hero. Both guys engaged the audience deeply, and their bouts were full of drama and passion. In the ring, their conflict demonstrated their ability to weave gripping tales, and their matches for the NWA Texas Heavyweight Championship rank among the most unforgettable in Texas wrestling history.

Beyond Kevin's personal rivalry, the Von Erichs had a significant influence on professional wrestling. They were a family who had a significant role in making Texas wrestling popular and in launching World Class Championship Wrestling as a prominent company. Together with his brothers David, Kerry, and Mike, Kevin rose to fame in the community and attracted large audiences to his performances. Fans were moved by their special fusion of charm, athleticism, and family values, and they went on to become inspirational and hopeful figures.

Tragically, a number of the Von Erich family's members passed away too soon, adding to their own personal sorrow. Fans' interest in the family's narrative grew as a result of these losses, which only served to enhance its mystique and history. The Von Erichs have had an indisputable influence on professional wrestling, despite their struggles.

Kevin Von Erich's legendary feuds with the greatest names in wrestling demonstrated his extraordinary skill and cemented his legacy. His accomplishments to the profession are still honored, and his bouts with Dusty Rhodes, Roddy Piper, and Ric Flair are still spoken about today. The Von Erichs' influence on professional wrestling is evidence of their commitment, love, and the lasting legacy they have left behind.

CHAPTER 6: PERSONAL LIFE AND CHALLENGES

Former professional wrestler Kevin Von Erich, real name Kevin Ross Adkisson, is most recognized for his tenure in World Class Championship Wrestling (WCCW) in the 1980s. He was born in Belleville, Illinois, on May 15, 1957. Out of his six brothers, he is the second oldest and became a professional wrestler. Fritz Von Erich, the father of Kevin, was a professional wrestler and promoter.

Tragic events and difficulties have characterized Kevin's personal existence. At the age of 25, David, his younger brother, passed away from acute enteritis in 1984. His brother Mike committed suicide in 1987 as a result of this. Tragically, so did his two brothers, Chris and Kerry. In 1991, Chris overdosed on drugs and died, and in 1993, Kerry killed herself.

In spite of these tragedies, Kevin has persevered and been a great role model in the wrestling world. He has four children along with his wife Pam, whom he married in 1980. Though it wasn't always simple, Kevin was able to find a way to combine his family and wrestling career.

In 1976, Kevin entered the WCCW, his father's business, to start his professional wrestling career. He was well-known for his agility and daring maneuvers, and he swiftly gained popularity. The NWA American Heavyweight Championship and the WCCW World Heavyweight Championship are only two of the many titles he earned throughout his career.

Kevin always prioritized his family above his career in the ring. When he was at home, he made sure to spend time with his kids and would often take them to wrestling matches. In order to be with his family for significant occasions, like his children's births, he also made sure to take time off from wrestling.

Kevin has been active in a number of humanitarian projects in addition to his job as a wrestler. He has raised funds for cancer research via his involvement with the Make-A-Wish Foundation. Along with being an outspoken supporter of mental health awareness, he has also freely discussed his own experiences with depression and urged people to get treatment when necessary.

Tragic events and difficulties have characterized Kevin Von Erich's personal life, yet he has persevered and is still a strong influence in the wrestling world. In addition to being a devoted supporter of philanthropic organizations and mental health awareness, he has successfully balanced his professional wrestling career with his family life. He will always be recognized for his contributions to the wrestling community and for the positive influence he has had on many lives.

Struggles with Addiction and Personal Demons

However, Kevin Von Erich battled addiction and personal troubles for a very long time behind the glamor and flash of the wrestling industry. His struggle with misfortune and path to redemption is proof of the resilience of the human spirit.

Being the son of a well-known character in the wrestling business, Fritz Von Erich, Kevin grew up in a family steeped in the sport. Kevin was born to follow in his father's footsteps, as were his brothers, Kerry, Mike, Chris, and David. In Texas, the Von Erichs were well-known and had great success in the professional wrestling industry.

Kevin, however, suffered with the burden of carrying on the family heritage. He suffered with expectations weighing him down and thoughts of inadequacy. Kevin resorted to drink and drugs as a coping mechanism for these feelings, finding momentary relief from his suffering in these substances.

His addiction became out of hand, which caused his personal and professional life to take a nosedive. Kevin lost his greatest performance and became unreliable, which hurt his wrestling career. Tragically, Kevin's brothers, Chris, Mike, and David, all died at a young age, shrouding the once bright future of the Von Erich family.

Kevin's addiction and inner troubles were further made worse by the death of his siblings. He battled to find purpose in his own life and had survivor's guilt. His drug problems were only made worse by the wrestling business, which is notorious for its hard schedule and party atmosphere.

But in the middle of the night, Kevin saw a ray of light. He got to know Pamela, the woman he would marry, and she helped him along the way to atonement. Kevin started to seek therapy and face his addiction head-on with her love and support.

Kevin did not have an easy comeback. Along the road, he had several failures and relapses. Nonetheless, he gradually began to reconstruct his life with the help of his family and the wrestling world. He started going to therapy sessions, got aid from a specialist, and adopted a better lifestyle.

Kevin's religion provided him comfort as well. He sought solace in the idea that he might conquer his inner demons by turning to religion as a source of support and direction. His rehabilitation was fueled by his faith, which gave him a sense of direction and significance in life.

Kevin was able to recover from his addiction and start again over time. He started advocating for addiction treatment and used his own experience to uplift others facing similar struggles. Utilizing his position, he spread the word about the risks associated with drug usage and the need of getting treatment.

Kevin Von Erich is a modern-day embodiment of resiliency and atonement. He's achieved inner peace and has repaired his ties with his family. Even though his history will always leave scars, Kevin has learnt to accept his challenges as a necessary part of his path to self-improvement.

Kevin's narrative serves as a reminder that redemption is always possible, despite the depth of one's problems. Adversity may be overcome and a better future can be found with perseverance, support, and a readiness to face inner demons. The life of Kevin Von Erich is a monument to the strength of the human spirit and its ability to evolve and change.

CHAPTER 7: RETIREMENT AND LIFE AFTER WRESTLING

When Kevin started wrestling in 1976, he gained a lot of popularity among the audience. His abilities to engage the crowd and do acrobatics were well-known. The NWA American Heavyweight Championship, the NWA Texas Heavyweight Championship, and the WCCW World Heavyweight Championship are just a few of the titles he earned throughout his career.

Unfortunately, injuries ended Kevin's wrestling career. He had a neck injury in 1993, which forced him to stop from wrestling. After the injury was fixed surgically, the physicians recommended that he give up wrestling to prevent further harm to his neck.

Kevin put his family and his beliefs first when he gave up wrestling. After experiencing a spiritual awakening, he set out to spread his story around the globe. In addition, he established a ranch in Hawaii where he kept cattle and horses with his family.

Kevin made his one and only wrestling comeback in 2009. He faced the squad of Brett Wayne Sawyer, Sigmon, and Matt Riviera with his sons Ross and Marshall. Kevin's late brothers, David, Kerry, and Mike, were honored in a bout that was held at the NWA Legends Fanfest in Charlotte, North Carolina.

Kevin hasn't stopped putting his family and religion first after he left the wrestling arena. "Wrestling with the Devil: The True Story of a World Champion Professional Wrestler - His Reign, Ruin, and Redemption," a book he wrote detailing his life both inside and outside the ring, is that account. In addition, he has spoken with fans about his experience at wrestling conventions and events.

Due to injuries, Kevin Von Erich had to retire from professional wrestling; nevertheless, he has since found contentment in his religion and family. He has shared his story and written a book about his life as he has adjusted to life away from the ring. Even though Kevin left the world of professional wrestling, his reputation as a fan favorite and a part of the Von Erich wrestling family will live on.

Kevin's Contributions to the Wrestling Industry

Kevin had a tremendous effect on the wrestling business as a member of the illustrious Von Erich family, influencing next generations of wrestlers and establishing a long-lasting legacy.

Kevin started his career in wrestling in the late 1970s when he signed up for World Class Championship Wrestling (WCCW), the organization run by his father Fritz Von Erich. Kevin became a vital component of the promotion's success, along with his brothers David, Kerry, Mike, and subsequently Chris. The Von Erich brothers captured the hearts of wrestling fans all around the globe with their charm, physical prowess, and attractive appearance. They became fan favorites very fast.

Kevin's in-ring efforts were among his most significant achievements to the wrestling business. He had a unique combination of technical proficiency, aerial acrobatics, and unmistakable audience engagement. Fans were often on the edge of their seats during Kevin's bouts because they were so intensely emotional and high-energy. He distinguished himself from his colleagues with his ability to tell a tale in the ring and elicit genuine emotions from the audience.

It is impossible to exaggerate Kevin's influence on the next generation of wrestlers. He impacted many wrestlers that followed him with his unique style and moveset. Numerous professional wrestlers, including Daniel Bryan, Bret Hart, and Shawn Michaels, have acknowledged Kevin as having had a significant impact on their careers. His swift and daring approach helped to shape the development of wrestling and encouraged a new generation of performers to push the envelope of what was possible in the ring.

Kevin's contributions went beyond his in-ring exploits as well. He was a major contributor to the WCCW's promotion and helped make it one of the top wrestling promotions at the time. Kevin's devotion to his work and his desire to provide high-caliber boats improved the WCCW's standing and attracted interest from fans of professional wrestling all around the globe.

There is sorrow associated with Kevin's legacy, however. Kevin was the lone surviving brother in the Von Erich family after a string of tragic deaths. Kevin suffered a great deal as a result of his brothers' deaths, both emotionally and professionally. Kevin wrestled and honored the legacy of his fallen brothers despite his overwhelming anguish. His ability to bounce back and persevere in the face of difficulty is a credit to his strength and character.

Kevin's influence on future generations extends beyond his work in the wrestling business; his family is evidence of this. Marshall and Ross, his sons, followed in their father's footsteps and went on to become professional wrestlers. They make sure that Kevin's influence will last for years to come by carrying on the Von Erich name and heritage.

The impact Kevin Von Erich has had on the wrestling business is enormous. His contributions to the WCCW, his in-ring exploits, and his impact on next generations of wrestlers have all had a lasting impression on the business. Kevin left behind a legacy of fortitude, tenacity, and a love of the game in spite of the horrors he experienced. Von Erich will always be associated with brilliance in professional wrestling because of the lasting influence he has had on both wrestling fans and wrestlers.

CHAPTER 8: THE VON ERICH FAMILY LEGACY

In the annals of professional wrestling, the Von Erich family is among the most illustrious. The family's extraordinary athleticism, commitment to the game, and tragically painful past leave a lasting impact.

The 1950s saw the start of the Von Erich family's wrestling career with patriarch Fritz Von Erich (actual name Jack Adkisson). Fritz played football in the past, but a knee injury interrupted his career. He then went to wrestling. He rose to prominence in the wrestling world quite rapidly, taking home many titles and ranking among the sport's most well-liked competitors of his day.

His boys were motivated to pursue careers in boxing by Fritz's achievements there. The "Von Erich boys" were the names given to his kids who went on to become professional wrestlers: David, Kevin, Kerry, Mike, and

Chris. Famous for their daring maneuvers and fierce rivalry with other legendary wrestlers like Ric Flair and the Fabulous Freebirds, the brothers gained immense popularity because of their exceptional skill.

Beyond their prowess in the ring, the Von Erich family had a significant impact on wrestling. By inventing novel maneuvers and tactics that had never been seen before, they also contributed to the revolution of the sport. The "Iron Claw," for instance, is a finishing technique that involves seizing an opponent's head with both hands and applying pressure until they surrender, and it is ascribed to Kevin Von Erich.

Tragic events beset the Von Erich family even if they were successful. David Von Erich passed away from acute enteritis, a rare intestinal illness, in 1984 when he was only 25 years old. At the age of 23, Mike Von Erich committed himself in 1987 after struggling with drugs and despair. At the age of 33, Kerry Von Erich took his own life in 1993 by shooting himself.

The Von Erich family and the wrestling community suffered a terrible loss with the deaths of three of the brothers. Their surviving family members and the many wrestlers who were motivated by their skill and commitment to the sport, however, continue to carry on their heritage.

The impact of the Von Erich family on wrestling is immeasurable. They were the forerunners of the sport, bringing fresh motions and methods that are being used today. Numerous wrestlers and spectators were impressed by their amazing athleticism and commitment to the sport. The Von Erich family's terrible history of death and heartache serves as a constant reminder of the toll professional wrestling can exact on its players, but their legacy will go on forever as one of the finest in the sport's history.

The Tragic Curse and its Aftermath

A tragic and eerie story that has had a lasting impact on the professional wrestling industry is the Von Erich

Tragic Curse. The Texas-born Von Erich family was once a well-known and adored wrestling dynasty that won over fans all over the globe with their amazing athleticism, charm, and commitment to the sport. Tragic incidents, however, tainted their accomplishment and permanently altered their trajectory in life.

Fritz Von Erich, the father of the Von Erich family, was a renowned wrestler and promoter who established a Texas wrestling empire. David, Kevin, Kerry, Mike, Chris, and Jack were his six kids, and all of them pursued careers as professional wrestlers. With their daring stunts, fierce rivalries, and indisputable brilliance, the Von Erich brothers immediately gained popularity and won over fans.

But tragic events befell the Von Erich family far too often. The first blow was the death of the oldest son, David Von Erich, at the early age of 25 in 1984. Although acute enteritis was first suspected as the cause of David's death, there were whispers of drug addiction and a possible overdose that spread around the wrestling world. His unexpected death rocked the wrestling community and portended the difficult road ahead for the Von Erich family.

The Von Erichs were plagued by the curse for the next few years. Mike Von Erich, the third oldest son, committed himself in 1987 when he was twenty-three years old. Mike had battled drugs and despair; his untimely passing shocked both his family and his supporters. The Von Erich family was left reeling from the unbearable loss of two brothers in such a short period of time, along with immense agony and sadness.

Kevin, Kerry, and Chris Von Erich, the surviving Von Erich brothers, wrestled on and upheld their family's history in the face of the tremendous tragedy. They put up a fierce fight in the ring, enthralling spectators with their talent and will. But when Texas Tornado Kerry Von Erich committed himself in 1991 at the age of 33, the curse struck once again. Kerry's death was another tragic loss for the family; he had fought personal problems for years, including drug addiction and legal issues.

The youngest son, Chris Von Erich, too committed himself in 1993 at the age of 21, bringing the Von Erich Tragic Curse to an end. The devastating end to the curse that had afflicted the Von Erich family for over ten years was Chris's death. Chris had battled despair and the weight of his family's sad past.

The wrestling community was forever changed by the Von Erich Tragic Curse aftermath. Five young, gifted people lost their lives, serving as a sobering reminder of the toll that pressure, popularity, and personal hardships can have on anyone—even the seemingly unstoppable. The narrative of the Von Erichs serves as a warning on the value of mental health, the need for support networks, and the terrible results of untreated depression and addiction.

The Von Erich family's legacy endures in the hearts of professional wrestlers everywhere, despite the immense sorrow. They continue to inspire wrestlers of future generations with their contributions to the sport and their unshakable commitment to their trade. The amazing influence the Von Erichs had on the wrestling industry throughout their all-too-brief existence is what really defines their legacy, not only their untimely deaths.

To pay tribute to the Von Erichs and raise awareness of the value of mental health in the wrestling business, initiatives have been launched in recent years. The family's narrative has been covered in books, documentaries, and interviews; these mediums have brought attention to the challenges the family encountered and the lessons that may be drawn from them. These initiatives seek to preserve the terrible story of the Von Erich family and to serve as a constant reminder—both within and outside of the wrestling community—of the value of empathy, understanding, and support.

One eerie episode in the history of professional wrestling is the Von Erich Tragic Curse. The sudden and irreversible death of five young, gifted athletes made a lasting impression on both the sport and the emotions of supporters everywhere. It's crucial to keep in mind, however, that the Von Erichs' legacy lives on long after their untimely deaths. In addition to inspiring and resonating with fans, their contributions to wrestling and their unshakable commitment to their profession serve as a reminder of the value of mental health and support within the wrestling community.

CONCLUSION

With the sun setting and the Lone Star State bathed in a golden glow, the legend of Kevin Von Erich seemed to blend into Texas's own dusk. A monument to the fights waged and the wins achieved, the wrestling ring, which had previously served as a platform for his athletic brilliance and unwavering spirit, was now quiet.

The sound of applauding spectators will always reverberate in fans' hearts, a chorus of praise for a guy who was more than just a wrestler but also a hero who stood beyond the confines of the sport and a symbol of tenacity. Not only had he made his mark in Texas wrestling history, but he had also left his mark on the international stage because of his barefoot elegance and Von Erich Iron Claw.

There had been some sadness and grief along the way. Royal wrestlers, the Von Erich family, suffered unspeakable setbacks after setbacks that would have brought down a weaker dynasty. Nevertheless, in the face of everything, Kevin persevered, bearing the weight of the family's heritage and entering the ring with an unwavering devotion and the affection of his supporters.

As his career came to an end, Kevin's legacy was not so much characterized by the cheers of supporters or the rush of success, but rather by the quiet times he took to contemplate, the respect he received from his colleagues, and the love of a family that had persevered through difficult times together. His defeats had been received with the respect of a real champion, his wins earned with honesty, and his wars waged with valor.

In addition to being a narrative about wrestling, Kevin Von Erich's story also tells of the human spirit and the struggle each of us has to endure hardship, rise to the occasion, and accept our victories in a humble manner. This story will serve as an inspiration to future generations, serving as a reminder that legends are created through the heat of perseverance and the cold of compassion.

When the last page is turned, the tale doesn't really end; rather, it just enters the mythical world, where heroes never really die. Although Kevin Von Erich's boots have left the mat, his footsteps will always reverberate through the passage of time, serving as a constant source of inspiration for those who have the guts to dream big, stand up for what they believe in, and live with a champion's heart.

Consequently, we say goodbye to Kevin Von Erich, the Texas wrestling legend, as the stars rise to take their rightful place in the Texas sky. Instead of ending with a final bell, his narrative leaves behind a legacy that will go on forever, much like the resilient spirit of Texas.

Made in the USA
Monee, IL
06 January 2024

51333416R00039